CELEBRATING THE NAME MATTHEW

Celebrating the Name Matthew

Walter the Educator

SKB
Silent King Books

dedicated to everyone with the first
name of Matthew

MATTHEW

In lands afar, where the sun meets the sea,

There lies a name, so bold and free.

Matthew, oh Matthew, with eyes so bright,

A name that shines in the darkest night.

From mountains high to valleys low,

The name of Matthew starts to grow.

It echoes through the whispering trees,

And dances on the autumn breeze.

In ancient tales and modern lore,

Matthew's name is heard once more.

A name of strength, a name of grace,

M
A
T
T
H
E
W

A name that time cannot erase.

In fields of gold and meadows green,

Matthew's name is ever seen.

It blooms like flowers in the spring,

And in every heart, it starts to sing.

With every sunrise and every dawn,

Matthew's name goes on and on.

It weaves through stories, old and new,

A name that's pure, a name that's true.

From starlit skies to city streets,

Matthew's name the world greets.

It resonates in every sound,

M
A
T
T
H
E
W

And in every joy that's ever found.

From ancient ruins to modern art,

Matthew's name ignites the heart.

It's a symphony, a work of art,

M
A
T
T
H
E
W

A name that sets the world apart.

In laughter, in tears, in every sigh,

Matthew's name will never die.

It's a beacon in the darkest night,

A name that fills the world with light.

From distant shores to home so near,

Matthew's name is always here.

It's a melody, a gentle hum,

M
A
T
T
H
E
W

A name that binds us, every one.

In every hope and every dream,

Matthew's name will always gleam.

It's a legacy, a timeless flame,

M
A
T
T
H
E
W

A name that carries endless fame.

So let us raise our voices high,

M
A
T
T
H
E
W

And sing the name of Matthew nigh.

For in this world, so vast and wide,

Matthew's name will forever abide.

In every verse and every line,

M
A
T
T
H
E
W

Matthew's name will always shine.

It's a treasure, a work of art,

M
A
T
T
H
E
W

A name that's etched in every heart.

ABOUT THE CREATOR

Walter the Educator is one of the pseudonyms for Walter Anderson. Formally educated in Chemistry, Business, and Education, he is an educator, an author, a diverse entrepreneur, and he is the son of a disabled war veteran. "Walter the Educator" shares his time between educating and creating. He holds interests and owns several creative projects that entertain, enlighten, enhance, and educate, hoping to inspire and motivate you.

Follow, find new works, and stay up to date
with Walter the Educator™
at WaltertheEducator.com